BLUES

BLUES

John Hartley Williams

For Paul
at the Voicebox
30. IX. 2004

Best wishes

[signature]

CAPE POETRY

Published by Jonathan Cape 2004

2 4 6 8 10 9 7 5 3 1

First published in Great Britain in 2004 by
Jonathan Cape
Random House, 20 Vauxhall Bridge Road,
London SW1V 2SA

Random House Australia (Pty) Limited
20 Alfred Street, Milsons Point, Sydney,
New South Wales 2061, Australia

Random House New Zealand Limited
18 Poland Road, Glenfield,
Auckland 10, New Zealand

Random House South Africa (Pty) Limited
Endulini, 5A Jubilee Road, Parktown 2193, South Africa

The Random House Group Limited Reg. No. 954009
www.randomhouse.co.uk

A CIP catalogue record for this book is available from the British Library

ISBN 0-224-07344-3

Typeset by Palimpsest Book Production Limited, Polmont, Stirlingshire
Printed and bound in Great Britain by Biddles Ltd, King's Lynn, Norfolk

blue lagoons, crazy fires, sheaves of wheat . . .

CONTENTS

ACKNOWLEDGEMENTS

Acknowledgements are due to the editors of the following:

The Devil, Grand Street, H.Q. Poetry, Leviathan, London Magazine, London Review of Books, Poetry International (USA), Poetry London, Poetry Review, Poetry Wales, Stand, Times Literary Supplement.

'Freedom Zoo' and 'Magic and Peewee in the Rain' appeared in the Bloodaxe book *Double* (1994) and the translation 'Those Who Cross' (Abdulah Sidran) first appeared in *Scar on the Stone: Contemporary Poetry from Bosnia* (Bloodaxe, 1998). The translations 'Dissipation of a Fish' and 'Birdcloud' (both by Ernst Meister) are from *Dem Spiegelkabinett Gegenüber* (1954) and *Die Formel und die Stätte* (1960) respectively. An early version of 'Hungarian' appeared in *The Gift: New Writing for the NHS* (Stride, 2002). The poem 'Dan Dare at the Cosmos Ballroom' began life as a commission from the Calouste Gulbenkian Foundation. The first part was published in *Discourses: Poems for the Royal Institution* (2002).

FOX TO EARTH

i.m. Ken Smith 1938–2003

I have this vision of you, Ken,
                sitting in a pew
with a growl ready in your throat
                for the incoming congregation:
Leave the doors open.
                Could do with some light in here.
You're holding up
        a glass of pure spirit
to a ray of sunlight.
                Back it goes.
You turn to inspect
        the cross-eyed, the ruined,
the homicidal,
        and the betrayed.
They're stopped in their tracks
                by your regard –
vodka-quaffer,
        smoker in church,
hummer
        of a secular tune . . .
A line of them
        bump-backs up
to the aura of the door.
        You exhale and cough.
The sign reads:
        NO SERMONISING
but you'd give them one,
        preach them the time of the dog,
if they'd only stop
        that stealthy shuffle forward.

What have they come for?
      Where the hell are they going?

         ★

In Colombia they called you *Marinero* –
          it was your casual metre,
the roll of a man
      still following
his ploughman father's wake
      feeling the ridges and pressures
the half-stumble
      the soft and the hard
loping after the trudge
      of his father's anger.
No sailor, then,
      but you leaned forward into it
like an old romantic helmsman
      who knows
there's a story in that port tavern:
      Matelot Night & Disco
with the girls
      from the quays
and not all the weapons
      parked outside.
You could smell conspiracies
      in the back seat of a taxi
read the minds of ghosts
      jostling for a view
of the grave
      life will tip them into.
And the dead floated down
      from a high rigging
like ethereal gulls –
      a slow leaf fall

watched from your window
    one Berlin October –
the souls, you said,
  of soldiers of the *Wehrmacht*,
hands outfolding from a sodden lawn
       and you
staring deep into the rain
    that reflects nothing back.
Riding the pitch and yaw
    of city streets
through the fret
  of storms and squalls –
nafikare necesse est –
  your line was plotted
to mirror the furrows
    drawn on your brow
by the need
  of holding straight
till you could turn
    the stanzas
as your father did the horses
   chomping and tossing
mouthing the bit
  on a wild headland
then plunging back again
     into spray.

       ★

I can still hear
  your half-American voice
dusted with Yorkshire
   a sniff of Cockney
menacing throat-rumble
    of a dog with one ear up

alert to intrusions
                freedom-ferocious
lurcher through language
                poached from the pavements
from rained-on roofs
                the elsewhere of home.
You caen't
        go there again, Jaahn.
OK, Ken.
    No need to harp.
Let's keep the subject moving
        at the forge of long conversation
blue archaic rap
        on the answering anvil
of a man who likes talking
        to a man who likes to talk.
Beneath
        your kitchen familiars
those onion bunches
                of gargoyle masks –
home-made devils
        state assassins, informers
Bosnians, Serbs
        los desaparecidos
maquettes of fiasco
        from the mould of your face
slapped out of newsprint
                torture-tight over wire
we'll talk our way home again
                        jiggety-jig.

★

Take this journey
        with me.

4

Let's ride the tram
        like lost speculators
through the deserted Bourse
                of East Berlin.
Let's eat
        pommes mit Blut and Schnee
from a cardboard tray
                with a plastic fork
stand on the broken half-moon steps
                of the ruined ballroom
read the graffiti
        scrawl-poems everywhere
on the S-bahn wagons
        on the asset-stripped yards.
Tell me again
        about that poet in Vienna
who threw his poems first
        out the window he jumped from.
Fumble with your lighter
                in the wind
remind me of the next drink
                before the sleet comes
and the tram's
        chilled faces
stare at us
        through snow-slashed windows.
Let's climb up
        into the warm interior,
have ourselves
        borne away, smoothly,
from what brought us here
                in the first place
whatever it was . . .

★

Borders? They say they're dissolving.
                              But are they?
What language shall we speak
                    across the divide
that unites us
          like enemies?
You said the border
              is the heart.
You paced its contours out,
                      sure-footed,
along the frozen edge
        of the mind's element
— *Voda Vodka Water* —
              a frosted pane
you'd snap off
        smear clean with a cuff-swipe
to peer through
          alive and inconvenient
a snapshot
      of the poet . . .
Your writing
          was listening
to a half-sensed audience
                  each thrown line
a flare tossed down
            at the sombre flood.
And this track I'm walking, Ken,
                      this border
that leads
        to a rough path's ending
a circle of trees
                no chiselled stone
no horticulture either
                just a hawthorn tree

to mark the place you're laid in –
                         let it compose
a line towards the break
                 memorial opens
something that won't
                 reach the edge of the page
something for anyone
                 something for someone
whose casual stoop
                 might read your name . . .

                         ★

Fox Running.
        The title of a poem.
Tea-stained sheets
    off a hand-cranked duplicator.
And along a border
            the shy, resilient animal
deserts the fields
                 for the city
hind legs stretching
        rusty muzzle in the wheelie bin
caught by headlights
                 scavenging shadows.
Dumb phantoms
            haunt the night-blown streets.
Between the legs
        of that cracked tribe
the perennial scapegoat
                 slips into darkness.
It barks once
        for the Courts of Justice
twice
    for the Mother of Parliaments

7

three times
          for the Walls of the City –
pursuit-baffler
          limelight-shunner
dog fox, fox
          poet, Reynard
the Drinker
          Reynard the Vanished.
Blank day breaking.
          Rain sweeping bald street.
Fox lapping from puddle
                    head raised
holding the look
          returning the gaze . . .

                    ★

But I don't believe
          that the fox
seen loping
          through the cemetery
as we carried your coffin
          down the weed-grown path
was anything more
          than beautiful coincidence,
nor,
   returning to your grave at midnight,
that the shape-shifter fellow
                    late vigil-keepers saw
was anything other
          than that same
interested creature,
                    sitting out the night
beside disturbed ground
                    with an animal's regard

for the presence of spirits.
                        I'd like, though, to think
that in a future
            long lost to poetry
someone in the tall data-streets
                        of an automated library
will find your poem
                    and feel the thrust
of a wet dog-snout
            into a too-dry hand.
As for the fox,
                    others saw it, not me.
Helping to carry
                your bamboo coffin
I nearly let go
            but hung on till we reached
that narrow doorway
                    in the earth.
You were too heavy.
                    And the arriving there
brought back a joke
                I forgot to tell you
which I'll keep in mind
            for the when, or the if.
How can those molecules
                be broken down
that have left
            these tracks to be followed
round potholes, bumps,
                    subsidences,
by survivors
            thinking of stories to tell
a connoisseur
        of escapades and scrapes,

one who enjoyed
    humour's darker shades,
Class A jokes
      is what I mean,
the sort
    to make an angel smile . . . ?

CAPITAL CITY

In city darkness, stone eagles
spread their wings to rise.
The tram squeals around a bend.
The driver in his cabin sits alone.

In lamplight's steady dazzle
the river is cold as the moment,
its current a bare, twisting rope.
The driver is attentive to his rail.

Over the bridge, it screeches –
an undulation in a straight line.
A single passenger gazes out,
brown hair glistening under the electric.

She has a rendezvous near The Gate,
at midnight, with someone
bringing packages for a friend.
The book she isn't reading has no plot.

Down the widest city street,
shops and towers vanish
into the windy night behind . . .
The tram accelerates.

She dreams her destination
might fly off as she approaches it
& leave her travelling, remembering
the reverie she does it for.

WHAT I ATE IN THE WAR

Clouds and red dawns.
Herbs: love-agony, death-sweet,
queue-grass and long-wait ataxia.
Ack ack meat.

The fallen horse of valiant progress
in strips.
Spinach leaf, cicatrice green.
Hunger-kisses from ruined lips.

Gall mushrooms. Revenge soup.
Disinformation pie.
Baleful droppings from barrage balloons.
Love thine enemy. Try.

Helplessness from upturned helmets.
The fuzz of doom
scavenged off the sofa
in the living room.

Silence siphoned from a tank.
Amnesia stew. Fever stodge.
Deserter sandwiches, stolen
from the knapsacks of the firing squad.

Rumour parsnips. Siren brew.
Acrimony from a rifled stash.
Bomber afternoons for soufflé,
after the flash.

Coastlines. The undrinkable sea,
the un-compôtable hills, the inedible strife
of wind and land, the searchlights
dicing cities like a knife.

FREEDOM ZOO

Now they've closed down Freedom Zoo,
we do exactly what we like. Though near,
in practice it was hard to reach.
Imagining yourself was what you had to do
before they'd let you in.

You checked on your reflection first
to see that it was tarnished. Their idea
of decorum was the drabness of your coat.
To show respect you had to prove
your shabbiness. They'd sidle up and hiss –

which meant: '*you're in*.' You carried seeds
to give the parrot. That grey doorkeeper.
The creature had abolished colour.
It perched there silently, a thing of negatives,
shifting on its claws of lifeless zero.

A rhino they'd experimented on
had died while trying not to think.
Heroic is the only word. They'd coated it
in monumental concrete, hung
a flag and sickle on its horn.

The penguins were encouraged by their keepers
to execute, by turns, a plunge
into a scummy pool. Each, as it emerged,
received the replica in plaster of a fish,
then shuffled back to join the line.

And in the petting zoo, they'd formed
committees of distinguished donkeys
devising ways and means of keeping
children out. *'No one's freer than he thinks he is'*
was written up in iron above the gate.

The last giraffe was shot for deviant views.
Dying upright, it had lain its cheek
upon the pillowed top of its enclosure,
and frozen yearning, with its eyes wide open,
was visible for miles upon the other side.

They'd be taking chainsaws to its legs
as you clicked the turnstile out. The parrot,
lounging on its bar, would squawk:
'Selected species will be released into the wild!'
Your exit visa had to be a sigh.

MAGIC AND PEEWEE IN THE RAIN

(title observed aerosolled on the Berlin Wall 27.03.90)

Like two lost conscripts
from the stationed eskimo army
hunting seal out on an ice floe
they drifted into the city.

They saw that someone
had broken the Republic into huge blocks
before tossing it into heaps. Left behind
were a few standing chunks.

They wrote their names on it,
first hers, then his. It was drizzling hard.
The ink began to run.
How do you spell it? she said.

His hand printed on her soaking shirt
the outline of her breast. They were lovers.
I watched them as I'd watched those walls calve.
Their embraces hurt.

They were the revolution.
I was the status quo.
They desired. And desired change
beneath a standstill sky.

By a last flight of the wall,
he pushed up her dress.
Something stirred in her throat,
a little tune of fuss.

His name. She spelt it with her voice.
First it fluttered, then soared.
He pushed her back, hard, against a picture
of a door flung wide.

Pinned by a gust, they clung
to the endless grey,
and were still. She eased down her skirt –
that universal gesture of degree.

He'd slumped into her shoulder.
Her eyes met mine.
Where would they go from here?
What would be the line?

THE DISSIPATION OF A FISH

('Zerstreuung eines Fisches', Ernst Meister)

Yes, that is Chaos: as a fish
appears on the table: Lunch.
Its eye regards the other souls, blanched.

Whole till now, quivering with life,
you lie before the hungry guests,
reviewed, decoded and assessed.

Once cut, apportioned, handed round,
the circle sitting round you is divided in you.
Bones and scraps are all that's left.

Even your remains, at last, disintegrate.
Released from everything, where to . . . ? Where to . . . ?
Cook scrapes skin-glue from a plate.

BIRDCLOUD

('*Vogelwolke*', Ernst Meister)

An evening
starred with starlings . . .
Were that wordplay
it also brings out
truth,
so blackly twittering,
an unheard-of-ness
in the labyrinth.

It must
be Autumn: a furrowing
of the brow,
the birdcloud
rising
from fouled treetops

to take
northwards, an
incomprehensible direction.

THE CLUB

Always the missing documents, the wrong money,
the neon-lit cubicles, the men in uniforms.
The dark panic you could smell
upon yourself, till you almost gave yourself away.

You had been trained for this. It happened, simply,
and they were the selection committee,
brutally committed to your failure or success,
which would happen, either way.

They analysed your obstinacy. It was dealt with.
They let you walk forever the way you seemed to want,
which seemed to be the right way, even when it clearly wasn't.
Predictably, you tried to correct your error

and caught their sly reflections in the mirror,
their awkward suits and damaged eyes.
Strange, stalk-like lamps flooded the pale concrete
of that area of uncertainty you stood on.

Expressionlessly, they suggested
that you should wear the star. Invisible, except
for the protection it afforded, it would be the useful badge
of your admission. Join The Club, they said.

You put it on. With time, wearing it got easier.
Like old clothes, it was proof you were you. Often, you thought
to discard it in the street, to loiter, watch to see if someone else
could see what wasn't to be seen, and pick it up. You didn't,
                                                        though.
Of course, you knew when someone in a lift,
or corridor, or at a neighbouring counter
had gazed at you for more than just a natural glance requires,
that you had been identified. And now

when people have been re-educated not to stare,
you still wear it. Are you the only one? It seems
occasionally as if a sharp regard has picked you out,
but you can't be sure. Now

the wind crosses these borders, without
interruption, the cubicles have become motels. And you,
who resolved never to let the obvious escape your lips,
never to fill in forms legibly . . . you're still here.

Are you longing for that cold glove to rest again, lightly,
on your neck? Passing some deserted barrack, through which
the winter gusts slide, does a kind of yearning seize you
for those papers blowing round the dusty floor?

There are no procedures, they explained,
for resignation from The Club. Its members, anyway,
will remain invisible to one another. And thus,
you too can walk towards the centre, stand alone

upon the square the missing statue occupied,
conjure up its overcoat of bronze, those towering folds,
and raise your glance toward the greyness of a sky
turning imperceptibly to rain.

FOR MILICA

Are our boys doing a grand job?
I suspect they are, Milica.
Is *Svetozara Markovića* quiet?
Does the waiter still limp in the *Gurman*?
Has Čika Ivan lit the stove in the classroom?
What shall I tell my students?
I will lean my back against the warm tiles & say:
these planes do not belong to me.

27.3.99

I REMEMBER

I remember
that the Orient Express went no further than Trieste.

I remember
that the Italian porter, comprehending at last that what was
wanted was the train to Belgrade, cheerfully trolleyed the
trunk off the end of the platform into the night, towards
three unlit carriages from which the sound of singing
emerged.

I remember
how hampers of chicken, salad, bread were opened; how
thimbles of plum brandy were thrust into the stranger's
hand; how the trunk's contents were transferred into suit-
cases; how the trunk was filled with goods purchased in
Italy; how the customs officers, very thorough with their
fellow countrymen, did not bother with the Englishman's
luggage; how the entire carriage burst out cheering when
the officers left.

I remember
how flat the landscape was on the drive from Belgrade to
Novi Sad; how tarmac turned to cobbles at each village;
how wooded hills suddenly rose up from the road – the
Fruška Gora; how the road wound and climbed and then
descended through the fortress town of *Petrovaradin*; how
the car rolled downwards over the old iron bridge across
the Danube into Novi Sad itself.

I remember
that the correct position for teaching class, in a cavernous
room where a tall stove gave fierce, dry warmth, was with
one's back pressed to its tiles.

I remember
that an essay set on *The Most Remarkable Figure in History*
produced fifty essays on Marshal Tito.

I remember
how Stefan recounted the events of the battle of *Kosovo
Polje* – the battle of the field of blackbirds; how on the 28th
June 1389 the Serbs were defeated by the Turks; how every
Spring red peonies blossom from the blood of the dead
warriors.

I remember
that under the ubiquitous restaurant sign: *Glasses broken on
purpose will be charged at five dinars*, two men ordered four
glasses of *šljivovica* apiece and drank them swiftly, smashing
them one after the other on the floor with a deliberate
wristflick.

I remember
that on a bench, under a tree, on a hill outside the town, a
bulky red-faced man with hardly any teeth played bagpipes
driven by elbow-bellows.

I remember
how he opened his mouth wide, threw back his head and
sang slow-crescendoing, slow-falling ballad-lines; how
each cadence's dying perished in a whisper of vibrato; how,
vigorously pumping the bellows with his elbow, the singer
would recommence.

I remember
that street-vendors stood outside the cinemas with baskets
of assorted pumpkin and sesame seeds, crying *semenke!
semenke!*

I remember
that at the end of a film, the floor of the cinema would be
shoe-deep in a litter of expulsed seedshells.

I remember
how we all went to Sarajevo that winter, in the snow.

I remember
that the Vrelo Bosne – source of the river Bosna – boils out
of the rock through two nostril holes at the foot of Mount
Igman.

I remember
that the force of the water creates a criss-cross pattern of
streams, weaving through the trees until they finally join
near a wooden chalet and flow serenely away toward the
distant mountains.

I remember
how Aca Ilić remarked casually, as one might say: 'This is
where we get the tram' – 'This is where they shot my cousin.'

I remember
that in room 47 of the Hotel Starigrad in the old market
of the city, there was a sign above the washbowl: *Attention!
The pressure of the water is high and strong.*

THOSE WHO CROSS

('*Oni Koji Prelaze*', Abdulah Sidran)

To begin with, time passed.
We crossed the bridge and the road by
the petrol station, and there
reasonably enough it said: No Smoking,
so we crossed the road again, with
hesitant steps, under Trebevic, fearing
change, a sudden shower.

>Dead air. A stone. A snake.
>The frozen chlorophyll of Toledo.
>*Españoles sin patria.*

Afterwards, time passed. We looked
one another in the eyes, summing it up for
the thousandth time. How shall we root out
the heart of this sadness? Someone
had left us. Yahweh will be alone again.

>*ombre prejudo y entelegente*
>*lavrador publico dija i tarde*

Then time passed. We climbed
the stairway, not counting the steps, to the stone
quadrature (here lies the one who has departed)
**Jasenovac, Gradiška, Djakovo, Jadovono,
Loborgrad, Auschwitz, Bergen-Belsen,** peace.

>*Clara, no lloras hija mia,*
>*no temes la fosa fria.*

And further time passed. Down below,
was dona Clara in a bikini, the marks of indolence
strewn around her head: *die Sonnenbrille*, 'Elle',
and there a *Feuerzeug*, cigarettes, a little music box
from Japan. A heart has stopped beating.

>   *Muy presto te perdimos*
>   *caro padre amoroso*
>   *yece con nuesta madre*
>   *en eterno reposo.*

The world's a torch, burning
at both ends. Thus we are alone – the living, the dead –
always the same. Is Elohim crying?
Adonai whimpering? Here, for a long time, no one
has cut the grass or the weeds. Only the limes flower
and the walnut ripens. The earth is clean, unblemished.

>   *Madre que non conoce otra justicia*
>   *que el perdon ni mas ley que amor.*

You who have crossed that final
highway, sleep. Let time go by. Sleep,
and time will cease. Sleep, for nothing
will be and nothing will ever have been.
Sleep, for the sky remembers nothing. There is only
Nothing, a black hole. Nothing Which Flows
To A Black Hole
Which
Grows

Note: the mediaeval Spanish in this poem (Ladino) is a reminder that many sephardic Jews found a home in Sarajevo. The title of the poem alludes to the word Hebrew, said to derive from the verb 'abhar' meaning *to cross over*.

SLOBODAN

In his chair of Marxist baroque,
he swivels from face to face.
What he denies, he denies.
What he admits, he admits.

A field of blackbirds
burns in his obstinate mind.
A tram-pole's flash
recedes along the night.

He yearns for a purer malice,
for a leopard shirt of names.
The ruinous song of defeat
stales in his lethal hair.

12.4.99

SARAJEVO DANCING

When you have drunk the mud-coffee,
been overpowered by the lushness
of baklava steeped in honey,
walked along Vojvode Stepe Obala
beside the Miljačka –
simply stand in Princips' footsteps:

the Archduke will come towards you,
his great face hanging,

>   huge-cheeked, bushy-
>   eyebrowed, murderous fool of the state . . .

>   Offer him strawberry *slatko*, a small bowl of *ratluk*,
>   sweetness. Offer him reason.

At your back
the Miljačka is flowing.

You are in Baščaršija.
Buy a fez. Or a fur hat. Wear it.
Buy a *džezva* for your tiny cup of mud.

>   Tinsmiths and silversmiths.
>   Pastry cooks and cobblers.

In the courtyard of the mosque
of Gazi Husref Bey, trees set in cobblestones
stand full-leafed above the fountain.
Water trickles the endless rumours
of water. She is smiling,
the muezzin's daughter

with whom I danced, not seeing
the feral shadow in the corner,
her bitten-off left hand . . .

Five times her father
called to prayer the faithful.
In counterpoint, another song
unwound its lament:

'She rose early, the girl from Kosovo
She rose early, on a Sunday . . .'

as we whirled
        in that *kolo*
gripping each other by the belt
joined by hand
        or clasped hand and arm

            accordion and violin
            slapping the air
            feet moving, the eye can't follow them,
            dancing . . .

And I heard
the cool voice of the Belgrade announcer
Dvadeset časova: Vesti:

Lazar, the choice is yours:
a heavenly or an earthly kingdom . . .

And in place of earthly victory at Kosovo,
Lazar has chosen God . . .

'We use the potato peeler
on the rough spots,' says the radio.

Terrified, in dark hotels,
the tourists lie awake, listening . . .

> And in another room
> one after another the soldiers
> rip the bloomers off Muslim women

and I saw
the white face of the Serbian leader
crouched over their naked backs,
an opened oyster of death

> as I danced with her to the words
> that took her father by the throat:

> > *Uranila Kosovka devojka*
> > *Uranila rano u nedelju*

> that they played in the hills
> to those dying on the blackbird field
> who were reconstituted as men
> got up and walked
> were slain again
> lay down in blood and bones
> interminably fixed there
> by the tune . . .

And as we danced they drove the stake
into the anus of her father, through his body, avoiding
the vital organs, until it emerged
near his neck, and so left him,
several days

as we whirled
in that *kolo*
gripping each other by the belt
wild tempo to
jubilant climax.

The street cracks open. Past
the Hotel Starigrad
the old Washington DC tram moves and in slow motion
derails. The
leviathan
emerges . . .

Muslim girls magnetise its snout,
shuddering up from burning asphalt,
and they struggle
not to look at its body

the sex

it caresses with foaming tongue
stitching their stare to its own

and you turn your eyes to where,
dancing, each one gazes on the other
feet moving fast, now together, now apart
permanent vibration
skip, tap, shudder through the whole body
whole circle of the dance electrified
accordion, violin and stamping bass . . .

PUT THE GRAVES ON STILTS . . .

Put the graves on stilts, so frogs can't jump that high
Put the graves on stilts, so frogs can't jump that high
Here comes the band, they need an alibi

This tune's a wagon, the driver knows the round
This tune's a wagon, the driver knows the round
How many potholes, chief, before we all go down?

Quicken that tempo, march me to the truth
Quicken that tempo, march me to the truth
Open up the rumpus room, give my yearnings oomph

Thoughts to the devil, hope a dead flambeau
Thoughts to the devil, hope a dead flambeau
Before the dance begins, tilt them your chapeau

Bring me a glass of water, waiter; if not water, wine
Bring me a glass of water, waiter; if not water, wine
If I can't stay sober, it won't be for want of trying

Trambone's long glissando heal my grief
Trambone's long glissando heal my grief
Piano-player, soothe my disbelief

I've a loaded pistol and a polyphonic mind
I've a loaded pistol and a polyphonic mind
Show me the exit, leave those frogs behind

NOT TILL THE LAST
SAXOPHONE . . .

Not till the last saxophone's yawp
Not till the last wine's uncorked
Be almost sure the train has gone,
set off into the blizzard
with your townee equipment –
you'll get where you're going. Or not
Listen to the bass, like snowdrifts
planting traps for the mind
Tip the last of that bottle down
What was it: an '85 Pauillac?
Examine that sweet guzzle
with all the slaver of your palate
There goes the last train now –
think how impetuously you missed it
Have a flute sidle into your head,
an organ be your locomotive,
have it whistle at the stars . . .
It's minus nothing already
If you had a beard, zeroes would nest there
Your hair's a cap of ice
Keep your mental fingers in those gloves you lost
drawn now on a dark catafalque
by two steaming horses, to wait
at tall and peculiar gates . . .
The zish–zish of the cymbals
seeps into the afterlife of your pockets –
spray of an entranced dust
Moon's up. Train's gone
Anyway your thoughts went first
Flute's out, stalking the fields
wading a diamond ploughland
kicking thru crystal skulls

Chill factor, soul factor, song factor
And there's the night sky
patterned as a cloak is,
a decisive moment, no question,
and the train has arrived
where you wanted to get to
Be there already,
snuggled down, awaiting sleep . . .
Downwards, the hill points like an arrow
Snowflakes big as tongues
feel with a blur for your eyes
Stars are a Hammond organ,
solo hailstones,
hard on the roof of your head
Onward, friend,
to the town where eternity becomes fashionable,
where trains have not been seen in weeks
This is it boy. The blues
Hoist your bag better on your shoulders
Hoist that bag better on your shoulders
These are the long, cold, deepwalking drifts

IT'S THE UNWEPT TEARS . . .

i.m. Albert Nicholas, clarinettist

It's the unwept tears I like
in the song *Farewell to the Moth*,
written by Sam Feral and Bunny Marmoset,
those two lyrical wolfhounds,
their ferocious clarity of phrasing
a lighthouse sweeping circles
over the nothing typhooning out there,
sinking ships,
and anything else you can think of,
though I'm not particularly thinking,
nuzzling a second glass of *Veterano*,
enjoying its harmony
with anchovy-stuffed olives, and
absent-mindedly attentive to you, Albert,
the piping desolation of your high notes,
the gruff scrape of your bass.
Your circling strobe is nothing less
than the dark's animadversion.
You and the brandy sips.
But in between the rays I glimpse
things slipping past me
from the cryptic world of undoing.
Who are those enraged Pharisees,
crawling under the wires of lights,
to occupy the shadysides
of sunny streets?
Try another olive, John.
Another slurp, with something like
the breathy drizzling sound, Albert,
you make at the end of a chorus.
Ignore the phantoms.

And so, ignoring them,
I gaze at a lamp-attracted moth
bouncing blindly off the wall
just beyond the flicker of a gecko's tongue.
The gecko darts.
The moth takes a turn
no free molecule would dream of.
The gecko stops dead.
Missed.
If the universe has a brain somewhere,
that moth
is outside the universe completely.
And you, Albert – laying down
the freest of airy lines –
your *obbligato* to the bumptious world
makes floating counterpoise
to the dust-fevered
who mire the light.
You send old Crazywing
colliding off towards another candle.
Your sonorous contralto
quivers to its coda.
The olives are finished. So is the brandy.
The player clicks on to repeat.
The light rays start their sweep again through nothing.
And the gecko doesn't move for hours.

HUNGARIAN

Learn Hungarian, I must.
Open-air reaffirmations
of vows at the altar of discontent
are impossible without it.
Nor will the shape
of its exquisitely insulting thoughts
be visible until I speak it.
I have to master it –
have it slap the faces of critics,
germinate the seeds of family discord.
I need to groan in Hungarian
so Psyche can whisper strange solace in my ear,
so I can answer
with what I did not know I knew.

Hungarian?
This is, listen, it's difficulteasyspeak.
Speak it. Spit it. Seduce with it.
It's the oath-filtrated language of a cellar
burning through the mouth.
It's the finger of inhibition lifted
from a stop blown in a vat, releasing
a golden urine of the senses,
a glittering parabola across
the bunged-up barrels of the past.

Hungarian? It's what
the mob that occupies the castle yells.
It's an aristocrat, sweeping down a staircase.
It crackles on the auto-da-fé of its own idiom,
a vampire-silhouette . . .
At every primrose wayside crucifix,
deciphering its undead alphabet,

I feel the squeak of its articulations
like the swallowed tongue of a cruel yet devoted mother.

Hungarian,
guide me through the wasteland
to the bar on the corner at the edge of town
where moonlight glints off the eyes of wolves.
Lead me
through the plush curtains of my mind
which have closed off the proscenium of my thought
                                        for so long.
I want to walk to the edge of a light-circled floorshow
where thought is bared to its flame.
I want to forget English
for the naked challenge . . .

Hungarian,
your device is the cry of a waistdeep man
yoked to a snow-breasted dragon.
In your baritone profanation is the ring of battle,
a jingling of the tongue's accoutrements,
the tailsnapping embrace
of nothing at all.

Hungarian, I need your heraldic lingo.
Stiffen me with your rampant existence.
Restore to me the cryptic sorrows.
Make all manner of forays finally possible.
Become the language
imagining the rest.

CENTURY

. . . the map of England was a toy bazaar
Louis MacNeice

Terrible scene, August, the tram-driver in gloves,
hand-picked to go to hell, taking the tram with him,
the soldiers, their kit bags, the station clock,
the Accrington pals, the bomb primed and laid ready
                                        somewhere,
the handbag of pamphlets under the arm of the suffragette,
the fine Victorian beard of the copper with glinting handcuffs,
the miners in tweed jackets, on bicycles, playing football in
                                        the dust,
low voices and distant cries, to the general a whisky at 5 a.m.,
the clouds drifting and piling above the park,
slow hooves of the horses moving down The Mall.

Waiters waking with a start, like rabbits, in narrow beds,
king and country, a biscuit box that still rattles.
Now is the moment, now in the city, energy is human,
the imagination is divine, let us hope the young men will know
what to do with it. But the planes have streamed into broken
                                        cloud,
the barons of the air, with their scarves, are still engaged,
honour is a new machine. The engineers build it, their drawings
are built from facts, they finger progress as trains leave
towards valleys lost beneath dew, and they watch
in those valleys, their constructions rise like targets.

Airships would bring the end of the world, so thought Karl
                                        Kraus.
Silence is in the streets, the poor man pats the head of an urchin,
lifts his head to the faint stutter of turbines in the sky.
A nun in her vegetable garden dreams of profit,

the kind but cool scrupulosity of the foundation, the profit of
                                                eternity,
talk in the club chairs of St James's runs on predestination,
mortal words for the bricks of enterprise, the bricks of
                                confidence, solidly built.
In deep libraries under the earth, the readers are glad to be
                                alone, book in hand,
tiptoeing from phrase to phrase, from stepping-stone
to stepping-stone across oblivion.

Imagination is conquered, indentured to silence.
The crystal goblets tinkle as they are filled with wine.
The family is jealous, each holds a silver knife in his brain,
raised to slit open the letter of courtesies, to spill out the
                                                intrigue.
The villas rise in the mercantile streets as the people warm
                                                their hands
at braziers, on windy allotments, and pull the crumpled
detective stories from their pockets in which the family
                                murders itself,
richly and delicately, for the pleasure of those
whose faces glow, as their backs freeze, and the sun rises on
                                                columns
of marchers walking down from the invisible north.

The sport will recommence, the game of extinction;
the gambler is backing his losses, a vial of cyanide beneath his
                                                tongue,
cards greasy between tired, sweating fingers, he watches
and is watched. Beyond the card room, men fall out of the sky
                                                on fire,
cities burn the horizon, trains carry mortal freight to
                                ash-strewn railheads
where the deep-sunken thoughts of those who will kill

are the thoughts of the card players, unspoken in cigar-filled
                                                                gloom,
and the shadows seethe with assignations, and the personal
                                                    stink of betrayal
is a fog seeping from half-closed windows, and the radio leaks
thin bravado music, and the words have gone missing.

No one remembers it, not those who survived it,
and the funeral facts are surrendered, imagination gathered up
like a deck of cards at the end of the game, and the gambler
slips his vial of cyanide into a silver box for next time,
and the children limp down gutters finding pennies,
and the players go out on the balcony and look down the
                                                    century's valley,
a river of lights, whose noise was a measure of pleasure for those
to whom the noise was the thing, as it all boiled over, and
                                                            England
is the map they find they have unrolled, a map of words and
                                                            promises,
at which they gesture, laughing, and saunter back inside.

JACK DANDY

White limousine on the high top road,
rain gusting in from the sea.
Woman in a room, standing alone
in the house on the cliff by the sea.

Walking the floor, she dreams the face
of the stranger at the door.
With her velvet gown slit down to the waist,
she stops by the mirror in the hall.

> *Driving thru thunder,*
> *Jack Dandy at the wheel.*
> *Driving thru thunder,*
> *Jack, now how's it feel?*
> *What's it like in the diamond deep*
> *of your deep dream diamond mind?*

Stretched on the bed, hat brim down,
he never leaves his mind's hotel
till a voice on the line says: 'Now's the time
for tell-tale time to tell.'

What'll he look like? What'll he say?
She touches her breasts with her hands,
hopes that a little disarray
might make him change his plans.

> *Driving thru thunder,*
> *Jack Dandy at the wheel.*
> *Driving thru thunder,*
> *Jack, now how's it feel?*
> *What's it like in the diamond deep*
> *of your deep dream diamond mind?*

Down the glare of the road, his limousine.
His face you cannot read.
He drives by the coast, a calm-eyed man,
keeping down his speed.

Taking a line of grey cocaine,
she places her hands on the piano.
The rain is loud at the windowpane,
each silent key a hammer.

> *Driving thru thunder,*
> *Jack Dandy at the wheel.*
> *Driving thru thunder,*
> *Jack, now how's it feel?*
> *What's it like in the diamond deep*
> *of your deep dream diamond mind?*

Wet steps wind to the sea top house.
It's not an easy climb.
She sits quite still at the white baby grand
with nothing to play for time.

Piano lid slams, she's falling back,
smoke smell in the air.
Weapon in hand, he feels her neck,
strokes her tangled hair.

> *Driving thru thunder,*
> *Jack Dandy at the wheel.*
> *Driving thru thunder,*
> *Jack, now how's it feel?*
> *What's it like in the diamond deep*
> *of your deep dream diamond mind?*

White limousine on the high top road,
keeping to the limits of the sea.
Shadows in the mirror, curtains in the wind,
in the house on the cliff by the sea.

Deliver the message. Click off the phone.
All he has now is the road
and the rain and the radio
and the white line down the road.

> *Driving thru thunder,*
> *Jack Dandy at the wheel.*
> *Driving thru thunder,*
> *Jack, now how's it feel?*
> *What's it like in the diamond deep*
> *of your deep dream diamond mind?*

COUNT KOFF'S CONDUCTED TOUR

La beauté sera CONVULSIVE ou ne sera pas
André Breton

A kind of snot is blowing down the corridors,
skeins of glittery translucence, glibber cobwebs,
catarrhal fruit of chronic agues, bronchial *apassionatas*,
fertilising passive air
with germs of an encyclopaedic rheum.

A fever exudating through the tomb.

Here, the noses of my contagious forebears
snuffle on, encrusted in their frames,
the look of men about to handkerchief themselves,
scarves wound tight round thickened throats –
from too long staring at them, you could catch a cold.

Their dewdrops, fixed in oils, hold the code.

Prodigieux, n'est ce pas? Sneezing, they believed,
empowered their ejaculations. *Voilà* my paroxysmical
paternity who pricked the egg of generation at both ends
with sperm and spit together. How this mansion's
bedrooms shook from floor to ceiling . . .

I, progenitively, twice-enciphered being.

So this – *pardonnez mon rhume!* – is my inheritance,
a rumbling, divinating thunder-pain,
tremendous donkey-heaves, apocalyptic bursts,
with which I splatter panelled corridors,
soul-expulsions, luminous *éternuements*,

streaking venerable mahogany – where once it shone.

Through the lacrimating lenses of my eyes,
prickly sharp, the world takes shape: a target.
I loose off shafts of words at fissured-tissue pages
enacting with each bolt the whizz of origin,
transfixing truth in pulmonary lightning.

What is thought if not a ventilated brightening?

A poetry, perhaps? From wet,
from morass, quagmire, quicksand, the literary creature
rises up in pieces. With plops, it sucks from every boghole
facets of itself and in hardening darkness, full of tribal
cries and fires, it struggles to construct a world.

A world of you and me against the world.

Sense-transgenic interjections re-seed each
meaning's drift. Equivocally radiating blasts confirm
what lineage determined long ago:
you must surrender your semantics into my control –
the fellow who excogitates the primal sneeze.

My interrogations of disorder never cease.

Je suis le poète. Without me everything is lost.
Threat is piled on threat. Your language fails to exist;
it can't reciprocate the shudder in the form.
The world, as I refract it under mucal waves, mutates.
Control is decontrolled. The lines must be redrawn.

I offer you, *messieurs*, the physics of release.

LOVE PARADE

In her chilly northern womb, my mother brought me
down into the malcontented city
from a place where wind, on sheep-enclouded slopes,
creaks always on the mind, like distant music.

Its rawness drives the shiver through my veins,
that now, in deep July, lighting my cigar
before I push the Paris Café door, communicates
the icy message of anticipation:

a white-faced woman, fingers thin as claws,
who sits alone, will utterly requite my gaze – a look
peculiarly meant for me. Her chair is always vacant.
Just the loud guffaws, the babble and the fug.

Later, my friends. My mother would be scandalised
to see our boots upon the table. A cure for cancer?
Well, I'm listening, boys. Attentively. In me
you've one on whom you really cannot count.

Talk runs down. I stub my Cuban out, half smoked,
fling myself across the unmade bed and snore, until
a liquor-light begins to pale the glass. Dawn.
My brandy-driven, tree-branched reverie is lopped

to pieces. A million-headed, sweat-exchanging,
honky-tonking, flagrant, semi-naked defilade,
hammered forward to an axe-blow beat,
is bouncing inch by inch along the boulevard below.

Loudspeakers beat the rabbits' brains out in the park.
Couples couple in the bushes. Are those human cries
floating through the ether, on pile-driving heartbeats?
On every inch of skin, tattoos proclaim the end of war.

In the dusty, 4th floor window-pane, something glows
around my own reflection. The silent circle of a howl
invades my mind. A trembling match I hold
to my cigar-stub ignites the room in smoky rivers.

Pure force of water scatters shadows in its torrent.
Heavy-waisted, to the city down that track, my mother
swung me, awkward, from the hips, over stepping-stones
across the deep dissolving silver of Black Beck.

14.7.2002

WHO IS JACK GILBERT?

*Put an academic poet on a platform with Jack Gilbert, and
he starts saying fuck*

Donald Hall

Loping to the microphone
in leather waistcoat and snood,
sleeves rolled so you can see the flames of a tattoo,
Gilbert holds a book of poems in one hand,
a cigar in the other.
Behind him on the dais, sits Herbert Tullivant, poet,
Mrs Tullivant, and the President
of the Little Chutapawqua Poetry Society.
Mr Tullivant is easing with a finger his too tight shoe.
Jack Gilbert surveys his public, lays down his cigar,
unzips the double-fly of his carpenter's leather pants, and takes
out his cock.
'If any kind lady in the audience would like to help me
engorge my piece, you'll see a classic work of the tattooists's
art!'
The fever of a silence contaminates the room.
Gilbert puts away his member and growls back at Tullivant:
'Time was, the front row would have gotten pissed on for that!
Am I getting polite, or what? Ain't nobody bought me a
drink, yet!'
He introduces his first poem, an unfinished sequence.
The way he says 'unfinished' makes it sound a threat.
The poem's about being horny in Central Park, New York.
Finding a young man asleep from too much alcohol, beneath
a bush,
Jack Gilbert undoes the young man's pants, and slips his dick
into a very relaxed anus, comes with a thrilling curse,
and the young fellow turns over in surprise
and Gilbert kisses him full on the lips.

The poem is called 'Strange Meeting' and Gilbert reads it
energetically.
It contains ten uses of the word 'fuck', six uses of the word
'asshole',
and the expression 'feeling a turtle', whose meaning
most of the audience feels slightly sick to guess at.
'Like that one, Herb?' asks Jack.
Herb hardly hears the question. He's staring at his poems.
Suddenly, and unaccountably, they appear to have been typed
in Cyrillic.
Mrs Tullivant, who usually never listens at readings,
looks as if she's just woken from a terrible dream.
The President of the Little Chutapawqua Poetry Society is
studying
the red fire extinguisher on the wall.
The next poem in Jack Gilbert's sequence is called 'Revenge'.
The young man, waking, realises what has happened to him,
beats Jack Gilbert up, and steals all his clothes.
So there's our Jack, mother-naked in Central Park, New York,
on a warm September evening. He sets off down the grassy
slope,
wrapping himself in a mental blanket, to look for a real one.
The audience doesn't laugh. 'That's supposed to be funny,'
Jack interjects
into the flight of his poem, 'why the fuck don't you laugh?'
On his way over the tufted ground, he encounters two Mayan
indians.
In the light of a candle, performing a weird ritual, they are
about to eat an enormous mushroom.
'Magic mushroom?' asks Jack. He is invited to partake.
The indians show no surprise at his nudity.
Chewing on his mushroom, Jack has a vision of his mother
with four breasts and a rat hanging by the teeth on each
nipple.

Jack spits out the mushroom, takes a deep breath, and says
                                                    what he saw.
'You fucking poser,' says one of the indians, this time in a
                                                    normal accent,
'you just ate an ordinary field mushroom.'
Jack Gilbert is enraged.
He knocks out one of the indians. The other one runs away.
From his unconscious insulter, he steals
a drab hempen shift, a multi-coloured poncho, foot-thongs, a
                                                    straw sombrero,
and lopes off back to Manhattan.
He squats in the shadow of a high building and puts his hat
                                                    on the floor.
In three hours he collects
eight dollars forty cents, three escuderos, two pound coins, a
                                                    number of deutschmarks,
something that looks like a yen, a kopek, maybe, a variety of
                                                    pesos.
The life of a poet, concludes Jack, is fortuitous, gratuitous and
                                                    somewhat circuitous.
Herbert Tullivant is beginning to feel he's been abducted by a
                                                    tattoo.
The members of the Little Chutapawqua Poetry Society are
                                                    thinking of their own haiku.
They're wondering if what they have risked for art was worth it.
But now, Jack is on to the third poem of his sequence, called
                                                    'What Happened Next?'
'I fell asleep, that's what. Fell asleep on the street,
and nobody mugged me or stole my takings,
whaddaya think of that?'
The audience isn't sure. Is this a call-and-response sort of a
                                                    poem?
'So here comes the mornings-in-Manhattan-crowd, they're
                                                    very generous.
And whaddaya think of this? Airplanes!

Airplanes nesting in the tallest buildings on that motherlovely
skyline:
KA-BOOM!'
Jack Gilbert jumps hard with both feet on a loose plank.
He's a board-stomper, a rafter-ripper, a poetry ogre in
biker-boots.
'Every mushroom,' he roars, 'has magical properties,
and a mushroom, if swallowed, leads us irresistibly through the
maze of life
to the place where it happens, the event, the explosion, the
single, most gigantic headfuck you were waiting for!'
Herb has neither poems nor boots to match this.
There's a rumble. Under the doors, through the interstices of
windows,
through every aperture of the Reading Room at the Little
Chutapawqua Poetry Society,
seeps a thick, bronchi-clogging, stinking, venomous, abrading
dust.
'See you at the bar!' shouts Jack.

DETENTION

My head sports a cap,
worn askew, or not at all.
Its colour: blue.
Its badge: a golden tree.

I only put it on to doff it.
The cloth pill in its vaulted centre
is threadbare with scraping the ground.
Mostly, I just roll it. Stuff it in a pocket.

But what I get
for being caught bare-headed out of school
is hour long duress: Mr Wren.
He starts up like a tiger if I yawn.

The tree's a gospel oak.
The sort to which you'd go
to hear sedition preached,
and get your ashes hauled.

A mob flexes.
I see the lean, insubordinate grin of the preacher,
the mole on his jaw,
the single stump of a black tooth.

He fixes me with a finger,
calls me *boy!* which is only half-alright,
and sends me back to do my 100 lines again:
I must always put my cap on in the street.

I've done two, so far,
in carefully different handwriting.
May every sentence draw the lightning.
Mr Wren deals wolfishly with exercise books.

Those who did not fidget
have been let go. A dragon
dots each i. Swords cross every t.
The capitols of words are put to flame.

Has he forgotten me?
My flagrant lines
have crisped me nearly to a classic.
Mr Wren glances at his watch.

SATURDAY MORNING

The avenue fell from the sky,
a new avenue into which
                    the shoppers walked
unwittingly, gazing at the rich
window-vagueness of the dummies,

who lounged or lolled on what
might have been furniture, but wasn't.
                    And since when
had the shops acquired these names:
Wine, Thrush & Co? Donkey Venn?

At the doors stood sales persons.
They seemed tired, not eager, as if
                    they'd travelled far.
A big zipper ran up each person's left side,
which the shoppers eyed.

Nothing was said. The avenue stretched
to Cloud Street and the roundabout.
                    There you could catch
a zucchini-shaped tram, painted yellow.
Its destination: Fervour Market.

So many signs everywhere.
For Sale. For Sale. It seemed
                    as though
no one wanted to stay there. Or be.
And the trees were gigantic, in thick leaf.

Those who took the tram joked
about creatures hiding in the foliage.
                    As for the market,
that was a waste of time. Just a band
playing music that wisped like smoke,

and vendors crouching over
piles of red, green, or ochre powder.
                    Most straggled past
to the river beyond, and stared
at the winged ships alighted there.

Obviously none of this was meant
to happen. The lights had failed.
                    People had turned left instead of right.
Somehow dimensions had overlapped.
Everybody was very polite.

Inquiring of each other what they'd
come for, they seemed embarrassed to answer.
                    Something to eat, perhaps?
They were offered, grilled to a crisp,
thousand-footed insects, in baps.

There were little cries in the mouth
as people crunched them. Then the façades
                    blistered and peeled off.
You could see the old shopfronts,
proper girls with cardigans, a stinking bus.

I chose to walk back from the market,
clutching a bag of the carbonised creatures.
                    The trees didn't look as leafy
as they had an hour before, but I'd have sworn
that something scampered from

branch to branch, keeping pace
with the reflective displacements of my body,
                    and I was sure
it was matching my walk, unseen,
like congruence gone wrong.

It was good to be back
in the pedestrian precinct, with the bronze
                    ducks round the alu-tree,
and the sausage stand, and the signs everywhere:
Buy One Get One Free.

THE MULEFISH

The uncatchable mulefish
curls a lip at bait, stares out hooks.

Suspended on the pulse of oceanic tides
translucently it hovers (you can see its bones).
It rarely moves except to twitch a fin.

The mulefish is no prized morsel.
It tastes of excrement and daubs
(though no one's tasted it),
of bricks of electricity, of wrong-fermented wine –
a flavour, they suggest,
of the sweat of someone being crucified.
How do they know that? Certain is
that merely sighting it can rinse your mind
with suds of the apocalypse.

Whales avoid it. Sharks patrol another route.

Only humans, wearing aqualungs,
prong it with their tridents
releasing jets of mulefish blood
that blind them, send them
tearing to the surface with the bends,
or flailing downward to a bed of skeletons.

The perforated mulefish
sews itself with ripple-thread
from passing shoals. Falling, rising,
in aquatic nothingness it floats.

Every now and then a fin will twitch.

TRECLEGYN FARM

He climbed the ladder, past
the dangling lorry-tyre, up into the russets,
still unpicked. On the beach,
a girl was running with her dog.

Braced in the tree's fork,
he let the stillness hold him.
Dusted by apple-tree shadows,
the weathered gate below hung ajar.

Between the bumble of the world beyond it
and the silence, he slid away
into another world, where the garden
existed in an endless flow –

a corridor down which he went,
carefully back and back, fearing
the moment would cease.
How far was it to go

beyond a moment possible
in words? The sea
had ruptured into dazzle.
The dog was jumping for a stick.

Beneath him, like a diagram,
the fields were spread
into a venerable pattern.
In the stone-built farmhouse,

a squared-off monument to use,
a shutter rattled brusquely up.
The idea of human activity,
said Apollinaire, *makes me laugh.*

The feeling of the silence was a wave.
A gull-flock stormed the house.
The dangling lorry-tyre
moved slightly in the breeze.

ELBOWS

Between ouch and desire,
they prop the rugged thinker you are.
In a down-at-heel room, whose wallpaper is shadows,
they attach your chin to your heart.
Sculpture me is their motto.

Silent witnesses, they gravely pursue
nibsqueaks over a page,
following a scampering
down behind the wainscot of cognition.
They wrinkle in the dark.

Elbows. Teetering
on the verge of disaster,
or suicide-thrilled at an edge,
or rueful at the sharp jab of a door,
or creaking in the act of love . . .

When the beautiful collapse
has taken place,
they try again. Anglepoised
above the knowledge of the knowledge,
they shed no light.

Almost yet not quite broken,
familiars of the final torque and snap,
they haunt the opening crack of fate revealed.
Crooked cathedrals.
Eternity coathangers.

Most sombre of funny bones.
Secret gargoyles under Gothic sleeves.
Spades that scrape in earth.
Side by side, at last, they lie:
Cemetery wishbones.

GNOME LIBERATION SOCIETY

We were the founder members.
We glimpsed his red-lipped smile beneath a wintry
                                    apple-tree,
rolled him in a carpet, took him to the forest,
and one week later, he was truly liberated – gone.

That's how it began.
On ledges high above the sea,
in caves behind the screen of waterfalls,
in fields, on crags, in trees, we left them.

A leprechaun diaspora,
in stovepipe hats and daisy boots,
they dangled fishing poles, smoked ladybird cheroots,
shared tremendous jokes, carried buckets to a well.

They took to wilderness, like me to you.
You were my accomplice. You with the outsize shoes,
the grin, the spotted pinafore. We freed them one by one.
A jovial army marched into the dark.

Our revolutionary nights grew warm.
A silver net of moonlight caught
the pair of us, coiling, gasping in its trawl.
A gnome with bifurcated beard stood sentinel.

When day resumed, your pale face,
surrounded by the glitter of your hair, was still.
Your body rigid in a gesture of surrender.
For hours, I also did not move.

In the hollow of an oak, fixing
awkward chinstraps on your pixie hat,
I propped you up, and left you. I was thinking:
Whoever finds you, let him stand and wonder.

Now, I take the late shift. The sight
of colleagues hotly semaphoring news
reminds me of the postures struck by those
I see frozen in the homeward light of dawn:

One conducts a monologue.
One with ankles crossed, sitting on a bench, just stares.
One stands lonely, with a barrow, on the leaf-blown lawn.
One is trapped in conversation with a frog.

The fierce jig of one upon
a garden tub detains my eye – a snapped-off
fragment of my thoughts. To that paralysed abandonment,
I doff my hat and carry on.

ARCADIA

The glumness of the rooky wood
bends saplings into question marks.
The moon leafs back and forth. A noise is heard,
the pinging of a Chinese taxi-driver's clock.

Stopped to eat his noodles
beside the road, he's taken off his summer clothes.
Clicking chopsticks in the air, he jigs in bliss
to find how like China England is.

A dance to creaking sticklebacks
in secret ponds, to weaving frogs who score
an oriental music on their kraxing loom,
to moles who plot his gait with tumps.

Tresses of the shaggy bullroots slip
hidden visas underneath his feet.
Velvet owls hoot languidly, where
micklespit and puddock's whore embrace.

Down twilight's nude phylactery, he skips,
nettle-heedless on the ferny path
stars have painted from his taxi door
toward the mushroom kingdom of perfume.

It could be Wutungkjao or Shihkiachwang
His cabin light burns on beside a foreign road.
A dockleaf gleams inside his stinging heart.
China is his brain and England is his feet.

Who stops to scoff a noodle dish is boss.
Who belches warmly into cool, a king.
Who waltzes so priapically, a grand vizier.
Who, naked, weds a log, a sovereign lord.

SUMMIT

A hungry wind devours your breath
and there you stand: a pinstripe.
Here the artists used to come
in peculiar sunlight with nude women

dancing like feathers on each arm.
Imagination soothed their rue.
All day they painted love's abandonment
in cloud reflections dark on flesh, then

putting down their pinsels, quaffed
the mute Mourvèdre, the silly Semillon.
Below the cliff, the ragged waves undid
their simple notion of a clear line.

By fall of dusk, descending piny paths,
voluptuous with resin, shivering rays,
and treading needles, sumptuous and soft,
they sensed the evening's shadow taking hold.

The far sonority of waves switched off.
Forest silence struck them like a blow.
They pulled their models to the ground.
Foxfire raged at peacock's tail.

They'd painted everything desire could think –
but it remained to live, to sear into scars
with limb-entrancing scalpel twists, fever burns,
endurance like a canvas of the heart.

And you . . . ? You climb the torpid hill to see
what mangled recollection makes of this,
and stand there like a bowler hat
the wind will surely blow to Christendom.

ANKLE

Breeder of splendid children, climber of rocks,
you were the bounce in the spring of myself,
the axle of all my rusting exploits.
Who wounded you by leaving you undipped?
I watch as you stir like a dog dreaming.
Why do you revolve my foot as if winding a clock?

And why, without rabbit holes, do you give way like that?
Or, when I sprint for a train
telegraph *ambulances* to my brain?
Silently, on the tiptoe of reluctance, straight
past truths of repetition, you have brought me
to the cliff of question marks. And here I stand.

Ankle, I do not want to end my days in a cathedral
treadling sad spondees from an elegiac organ.
I have the urge to hammer out anapaests
and stand up to the piano like Little Richard.
I need to roam a wild beach and walk toward
the glory of the shadow without a thought of home.

So what if it's October? At your toe,
leaves are itching to be booted high.
Don't think about heaven in terms of miles.
Don't think about meaning in terms of shoes.
Direction is the secret, ankle.
You hold the key. Let's go.

MISS MELODY

Let us rise, then,
from the middle of your bed,
and clothe each other in white sheets.
Let's do the shuffle-step circle dance
and intone the bite-marked mantra
of dadoom.

Let me take a shower
in your gryphon-footed bath-tub,
the stem of its shower rose
so lovingly bedecked with thorns.
And let me carefully, so carefully,
turn on the water and watch it rinse red
while you dance wildly upon the tiles
in your gargoyle slippers, and giggle,
your golden mop protruding
from the body-chador of your sheet.

A barb or two will cling to me.
So, afterwards, let me stand there patiently naked
while you pluck them from my bottom with your mouth,
draw your tongue down my arse-cleft
and nip my scrotum fondly with your teeth
as a kindly afterthought.

Let us dance into the kitchen,
make breakfast of sultana scones and quince-rind jam.
Someone called Jeff will come shuffling in,
also wearing a sheet.
He will drip pools of water on your floor, and you,
with a vigorous up-Jeff of your fingers,

will dispatch him, and he'll traipse off,
closing your rubber front door
with a petulant thud.

All morning we'll watch the bank raids
on the *Highlands and Islands Mutual* across the street.
'How much money can you take from a bank?' I'll ask.
'It's endless,' you'll say, and flirtatiously flash
a silver-coin-capped nipple at me. My dearest,
I'll sip your bone-roasted death coffee,
gaze into your green eyes, the supreme dishevelment
                              of your ash-blonde hair,
your missing front tooth, and the sweet,
crazy curve of your shoulder, and think
of you as somehow being
part of a grand design that's trying to
exclude me, and
gloriously failing.

Let us waltz into the roman bath of your living room
in our jam-flecked togas
and watch the children's sex programmes
all afternoon. By four o'clock I'll be able to tell
if it's happening, and then I'll say:

'I want to play Miss Melody.
Have Jansen bring the horse.'

DAN DARE AT THE COSMOS BALLROOM

amor vincit omnia

(i)

Venus lies ahead –
ball of mists and disenchanted fruitfulness,
too hot for charity, too steamy for reproach,
my mission crystalline as snow:
to conquer what has always conquered us.
Airlock doors slide open. They reveal
the Mekon, president of Love Unexpurgated,
a peagreen Humpty Dumpty on a flying plate,
vestigial legs suggesting
toxic misadventures at the ante-natal stage,
the sonic scalpel of his voice
sharp inside my brain: *Welcome to the planet*
humans dream of on their cold blue ball.
Welcome to the temperature of pleasant being.
Dispel colonial ideas.
We've been watching humans from afar.
How could anyone invent a game like cricket?
An egg-sliced-open sort of smile.
I descend the ladder of the **Peril Two,**
alight upon the sighing ground
and contemplate across the rocket park
The Cosmos Ballroom, with its astral sign:
Pleasure Tourist Amorous Infinity is Yours
Without Regard to Species, Origin, or Sex!
'Unappeasable amour?' I ask. 'Is that your creed?'
No, no, the Mekon says. *Creed is what Venusians*
have never suffered from. We give no credence anywhere.
He loops a solipsistic loop. Even upside

72

down his saucer holds him firmly glued:
Venusians adhere – I use the word advisedly –
to two adjacent modes of love,
PARADISE – he points to entrance Number One –
or its counterpart: DISASTER.
'No human', I remark, 'would go through *that* door.'
Ah, the blindness of the Earthling, the Mekon says,
disaster if experienced aright
can be as pleasurable, indeed it may be more so,
than any mere paradise, whose quality . . .
and here the Mekon banks away, then comes zipping back,
. . . contains a level of inherent boredom
most Venusians, at least, deplore.
I jut my famous chin. Perhaps a man
of my renown should take disaster's door
to prove I'm up to it. This is Venus, after all.
My orders are to let the worst befall.
The Mekon has decided for me.
He nudges me with little bumps toward
a beckoning entrance, finger-fronded.
Through music that has fingers too,
notes that tweak my nose, and fidget
at the spaceworld issue of my pants,
tickled by the shadow of desire, or
seething with imperative, I go:
Now put on rollerblades,
slot them in this rail that weaves
a roller coaster tangle
over Consummation Chasm.
Keep your wits and balance, Dan Dare!
Lose your equilibrium, you'll fall,
and falling here on Venus is an endless process
that never stops . . . Suddenly,

I'm launched upon a steepening helter-skelter
in knee-alarming corkscrews.
Massed choirs keen from nowhere:
JOIN US! JOIN US NOW DAN DARE!
The tracks I'm on keep branching. I derail.
A thousand million voices rise in song
to greet the imminence of my demise.
I lose my spaceworld cap.
My hair's a streak of flying sweat.
Wafting from the nether world
the limpid ditty fans me with its coo.
Skates jammed firmly back on track,
high above the lullabying tomb,
I bend my knees to take another curve.
A fiery catherine wheel displays:
ENTER THE ARCADIAN MAZE.
Here each decision, counting down, leaves more.
I swerve. The signs read
NO WAY OUT, NONE LEFT, NONE LEFT.
More decisions, all of them superfluous.
The false deliverance of an EXIT looms.
Go right? Go left?
I exit into more decisions.
Can this one be the FINAL EXIT?
And then another one. And billions more.
Switch. Turn. Twist. Dodge.
I'm going right. Then left. Then right again.
From vertigo, the chorussing abyss
reiterates its roundelay of little death:
La-la again. La-la again. La-la again.
Then I'm gliding to the station where the Mekon waits:
I thought the famished roar went up
that would have signified
your transmutation to a morsel of amor.

Well, well. They'll get their chance.
Nothing here, Dan Dare, that's not discoverable
from one fissiparating body to the next . . .
Let's say this was
a little fitness test to get you in the mood for proper love . . .?
May I suggest a cup of sweet green tea?

Tea's a trial too.
It happens in the blue
Venusian afternoon.
Fumes of tea-room dissonance.
Disharmonies of steam.
In slanting mirrors on the walls,
converging to the roof,
misty nymphs demist and mist again.
The Mekon's eyes
reflect an alleyway of smiles.
Everything that's female in the universe
dawdles languidly before my gaze.
Accosted, I am twisted
on every eyebeam's fork.
Nothing for it but to play the hero,
sunset-jawed against the Cosmos Teabar's cockpit lights,
my hand on quivering controls,
(the Mekon is enjoying this)
steering wide of a universal mouth
that does not mean to kiss –
beautifully petalled rose,
beautifully petalled rose.
The tea's infused.
Everything is silent in the silence,
except the glug and trickle
of a samovar – Venusian green and gold.
Grey, metallic eyes
prise the Daniel from the Dare.
What weakness is, the Mekon knows.
Knows that he can make it crawl
beneath the sheets of anything,
with anyone, make it roll
into the warmth of any arms,

intemperately, anyhow,
melt its blood
with the icicle of love.
Tea?
The stuff I'm drinking
is inimical to sanity.
A barefoot vision walks into my arms
across a lawn of stars
and then again into my arms.
The Mekon clouds me with his breath.
My cap and jacket,
my air of resolution, smart appearance
struggle in a frame, like someone
trying to get out.
I crouch on luscious flanks –
the Cosmos Teabar seats.
Someone's standing in a mirror,
gradually unclouding,
our botanist, of course,
aboard the **Peril Two!**
– her forage cap unpinned,
loosened hair a waterfall,
arms flung wide to clasp . . . well, who?
Peabody! Miss Peabody!
Resist, desist.
My breath is thick as tea
and I can hardly drink it.

'This tea is stewed!' I shout.
'You slipped me Venus weed, admit it!
Enough's enough! Get me the bill!'
The Mekon's countenance
knobbles briefly – bestial kohlrabi –
then smoothes out irritation:
Enough is never quite enough.

I do applaud your mental effort, though.
How hard you Earthlings struggle to avoid
the inevitable! How little do
the outcomes match the effort!
But a simple bill is much too easy.
On our planet, we insist:
resolution of a debt is carnal.
His twig-like fingers crack.
A beauty, glowing green,
bald and sumptuously skinny,
comes gliding to his summons.
'The Queen of Waitresses?'
O no, the Mekon says.
This is Venus. She's the bill.

Venus takes my hand.
A herb-smell drifts through stars.
Love is anti-gravity, the Mekon says. *Ascend.*
A single room, above us, raised on stilts,
is entered through a heart-shaped door.
We climb the ladder to it, close
the door against his presence.
Undress, she thinks inside my head.
Her body's ocean in the dark.
My uniform's a pile at my feet.
I'm stretched upon a bed that whimpers;
she prowls across me on all fours,
her breasts crush soft against my ribs;
mournful thunder on the roof
prefigures thoughts of earthly rain.
I'm the single crewman of a craft
already lost. It tips
and I'm decanted overboard,
a downward-drifting pleasure-lode
through layered shafts of darkness.
She peels my lightness
from the stone it's wrapped around.
The part of me that's covered
by the part of me that cannot move aside,
released, begins to climb out free.
My blind hands read her every dip and swell.
And then,
a glow of phosphorescence stains the room.
The Mekon, cruising back, derisively
directs a torchbeam
at the knot we make, his mockery
a knife of virid glee. We hurl
a gale at him, in telepathic unison,

impart ferocious spin to his abominable frisbee,
and with a shriek, he flies off through the roof;
his dwindling shout of: *Having fun, Dan Dare?*
drifts starward
in a detumescent vapour-trail
of ice-cold jism.
Her answer to him, confidential in my ear,
makes me burn to hear it.
Her arms lock tight,
in olivaceous hoops around me,
the muscles of her belly
strain with inconsumable receptiveness.
She puts out tentacles. They slide between my ribs,
dote upon the organs they encounter.
My pump begins its agonising pump.
She slips a duct into my sac of seed
and instantly replenishes my emptying.
Once the circuit's made, she whispers,
it's unbreakable
until perpetual depletion's satisfied.
I'm a rifle jammed on auto-fire,
in love-mode, stuck upon repeat,
struggling to recall my training's first command:
alien sex translates to *harm*;
if encountered, personnel fall back . . .
I pluck her loving piercings out, like burrs;
she gives off weakening cries.
Love's machine runs down.
Something seems to leave me I reach out for,
hardly knowing what it is. It's gone.
The whole connection stands undone.
Dare and Venus –
soldiers that a war's rolled over –
lie quietly in lover's ditch, exhausted.

The Mekon, father of the storm,
rowing slowly from the epicentre
of the cyclone we dispatched him with,
examines me with saturnine reproach.
What might have been the sound of rain
is just an ambient hiss. Only swathes
and slashes of an inhuman hurricane are left.
Of Venus, there is nothing
but the ghost of an aroma.
The Mekon gives what might be called a chuckle.
Or something else?
I simply lie there: think of Earth.

(iv)

Behold, the Earth, the Mekon says.
Our reality machines run hard
to reproduce that scuffed-white sea,
the cut-out mountain tops,
all that lush geography.
I gaze toward the landscape
refracted through my fishbowl helmet.
So is it really Earth? And if it is,
is Earth a bent invention of Venusians?
And if it's really real
why am I encumbered in this awkward suit?
Where is Digby? Where the real Peabody?
Another test; another fraught descent.
I feel the throb of a lubricious dusk.
If this is their idea of us −
the only route is down.
I'm standing on a mountain peak.
And at the bottom: sea.
I watch its silver tracery
lining out in surf the anthracitic sand.
A few small buildings flutter flags.
Coastal dwellers move along a shore.
If anything below resembles
that cartoon you carry in your brain,
that longing of belonging you suffer from,
come back up and tell me that it doesn't!
A vicious cackle, followed by a yawn.
. . . Excuse me for a while . . . a ten-year nap . . .
He fades. He's doing it on purpose.
I train my glasses on a settlement
in a crook of gull-infested land
beside an ocean that seems real enough
and watch a carnival take shape: *The Day of Love.*

Before those stalls are taken down,
the floats dismantled –
is it there I'll find what I am looking for,
along the Avenue of Doves?
Or is the Queen of the Fiesta
a double agent of the Treens?
The oldest tree in Christendom's down there;
it hasn't moved a leaf since breakfast.
Midget dinosaurs are sniffing at my boots.
Is this before humanity, or afterwards,
or just the moment of itself, in itself,
despair and hope
cunningly imagined as a place?
Hard to say.
In the now I'm in, I have become a verb: to dare,
a spaceman-alpinist in monstrous moon-pyjamas,
climbing downward into sameness,
from frame to frame.
There my boots are at the top left corner,
coming slowly into view;
the branches I've dislodged are female arms
flung straight above her head, enclosed by glossy foliage:
a goddess of the cliff, madonna, sacred prostitute of the
    ravine.
The Mekon blasts me from his dream:
Disaster isn't vegetable, you fool!
I grip a ledge, securely lodge my boots.
My hesitation turns her back into a tree.
The noise of time is visible from here,
bouncing off the chasm walls –
an ear-confounding spectacle;
empty waves of previous millennia
crash on lizard-coloured rock . . . fall back . . .
above it all, another sign:
TIME'S NATIONAL PARK.

Human fate is stuck on an escarpment, is what I think.
The Mekon stirs and dips a straw
into the memory solution of my brain.
Intristing! he hisses.
Then he multiplies me, strands me numberlessly
in every episode of time, on every mountain top,
waving to my fellows on the next.
How will they interpret these unbalanced signals?
Someone happy to be toppling in?
Time to fall, Dan Dare. I need to sleep . . .
Rising from that avid vertigo,
the song he orchestrates repeats
its shameless, sucking-sentimental provocation.
I mentally invert its trash-seductive harm,
have it magnetise my boots
so I can get a grip again, continue down.
Do hours pass? Or days? Or years?
Fending off the Mekon's wild, contrary brainwaves,
I reach the carnival
upon the Square of Memory
where dancers leap and twirl.
Will they know me for the Dare I am?
Will someone say:
'Can that be you? Where have you been?'
A slender wrist takes hold of me.
I'm pulled into the thickening throng, begin
the clumsy hop, a spaceman's Morris dance
to music that is rhythmless and sweet
and hear the Mekon raving from his dream of malice:
You're wrong. So wrong! And wrong again!
How good the wrongness feels.
The one who holds my wrist stands next to me.
I take my helmet off, my suit, my boots.
I plant my ankles in the sea and breathe.

Where surf and swimmer join
beneath a grey, ferocious sun,
where paradise does not embrace disaster
but where their bodies move
improbably and equidistantly together –
divested of my mission and my clothes –
I feel the strict sensation of deliverance that comes
to any man, however lost,
who measures, paces out at last,
the lost co-ordinates of home.

A WORD ON DAN

Dan Dare was a spaceman comic hero of the fifties, invented by the artist Frank Hampson, first published in the *Eagle*. His faithful assistant was Digby. Miss Peabody was the ship's biologist. The Mekon was leader of the Treens, the inhabitants of Venus. The Mekon was a large green head, all evil brain, who propelled himself around in a flying soup bowl. The Treens were lankily humanoid, green-coloured, with lipless faces. The word Treens somehow suggests 'latrines' – echoes of camps, prisoner-of-war-camps, concentration camps, etc. – it was a very postwar strip. For satirical purposes here, I have given Dan a reflective, sexual being, not, of course, a feature of the lean-jawed hero of those long-ago stories. Readers who cherish memories of the *Eagle* will not find this poem unfriendly, I hope, to Frank Hampson's clean-cut original character.